We're off!

Pack your bags and come with us on a journey back through time. We're out to find the Righteous Radicals—a terrific group of Bible heroes.

What makes the Righteous Radicals so special? For one thing, they obey God. That makes them right, right? And they don't let anything stop them from following the Lord. That makes them pretty radical, don't you think?

Now here's the best part. We're not going to tell you who these famous R.R.'s are (well, there's a little help at the end, but no fair peeking). Along the way you'll find lots of other surprises hidden in the stories—you're going to be busy!

Put on your thinking caps and begin the search!

In Search of Righteous Radicals

SANDY SILVERTHORNE

Stories retold by
Karen Mezek

HARVEST HOUSE PUBLISHERS
Eugene, Oregon 97402

GET UP & GET OUT

I  was 75 years old and not exactly in the mood for adventure when God spoke to me. He told me to leave my home and my country and travel to an unknown land.

"I will bless you and make your name great," God said, "and I will make of you a great nation."

I had always considered myself a practical, down-to-earth sort of person. How could I explain to my family and friends that God had spoken to me? And what would my wife Sarah say? We were already old, and Sarah wasn't able to have children. How could God make of us "a great nation"?

But the more I thought about it, the more I realized I couldn't ignore God's call. Somehow, I'd have to find the faith to believe in His promises, no matter how strange they seemed.

I gathered my wife, my brother-in-law Lot, my whole family, all my sheep and cattle (5), and headed out of town. What a sight we made with all our earthly possessions packed on the backs of donkeys (5) and loaded into carts. Only God knew where we were headed. There was no one to guide us. We didn't even have a map !

But God was faithful. He led us to Canaan—a land more rich and fertile than any I had ever seen, a land flowing with milk and honey. There I built an altar to the Lord and thanked Him from the bottom of my heart. How glad I was that I had trusted in His promises, even though they had seemed impossible!

Guess who?

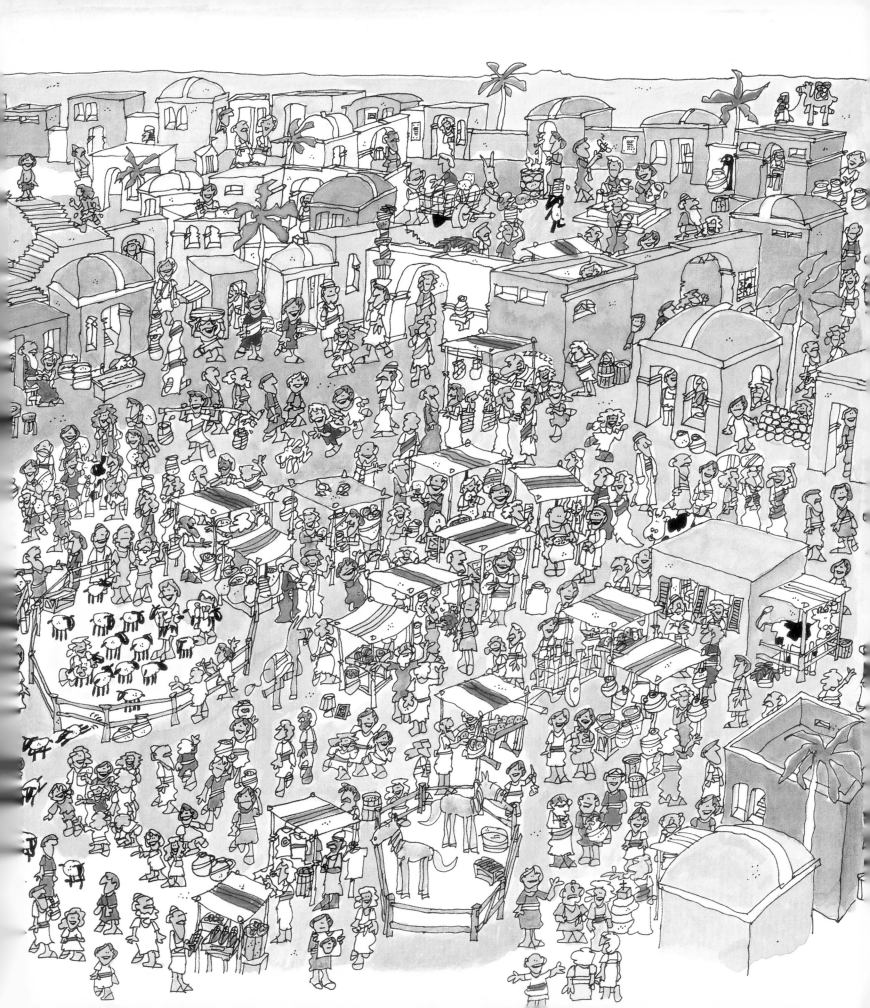

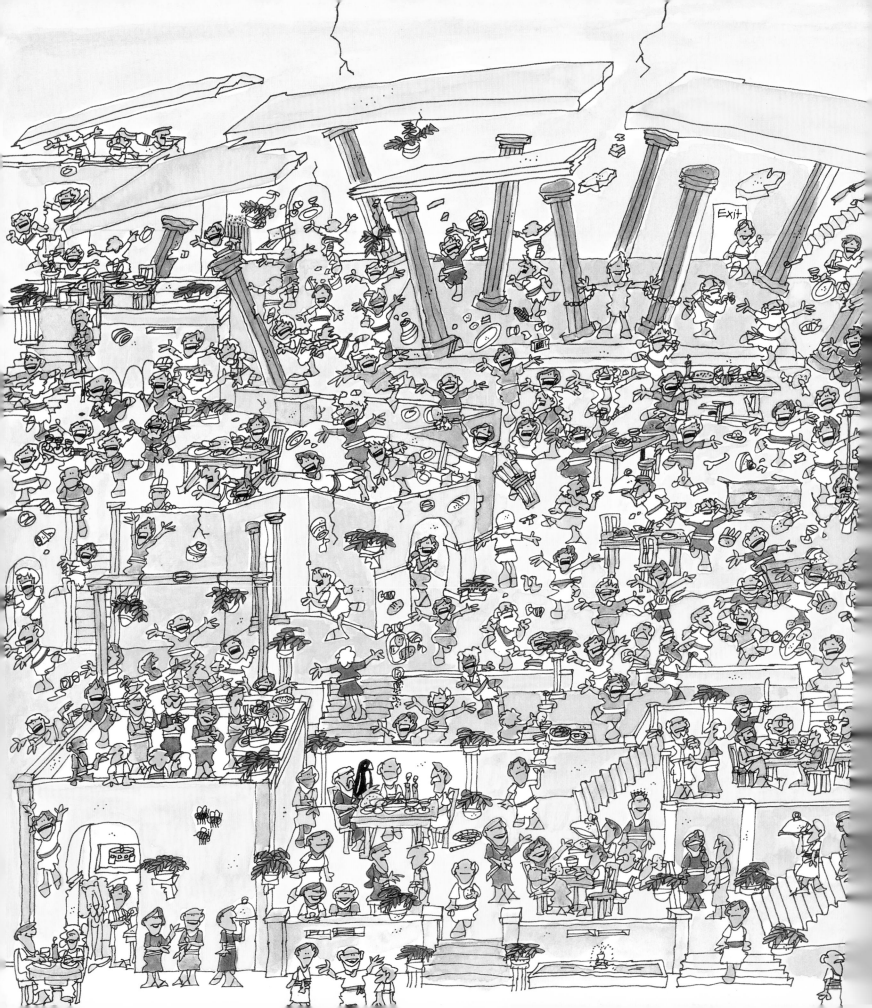

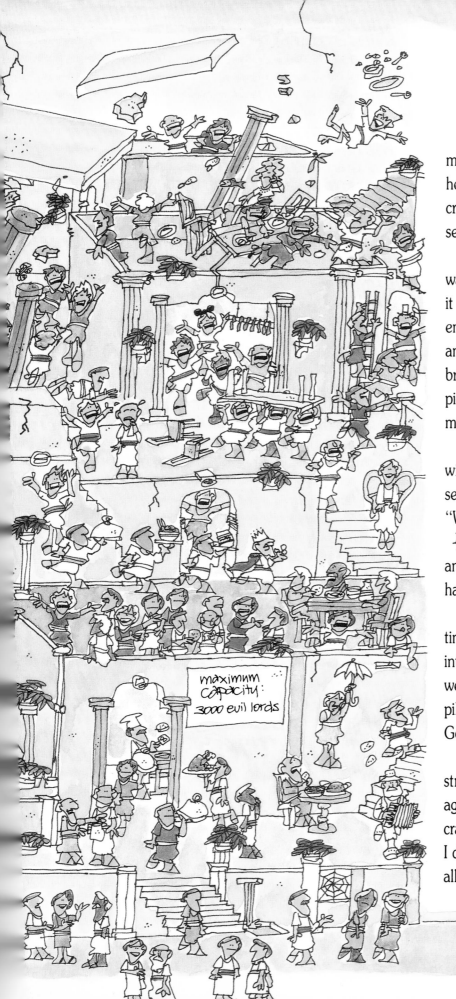

A SUPERMAN

When an angel  of the Lord appeared to my father, Manoah, and promised him a son, he knew that I would not be ordinary. He cried with joy when I was born. If he could have seen the future, he would have cried with grief.

As I grew older, I realized how truly different I was. Once a lion tried to attack me. I grabbed it and tore it limb from limb. Then when my enemies, the Philistines, captured me and bound me with thick, strong ropes, I broke them as if they were burnt flax. I picked up a jawbone and killed a thousand men.

My worst problems began when I fell in love with Delilah. Night after night she asked the secret of my strength. At first I lied to her. I said, "Weave my seven locks of hair into a web and I will lose my strength." Finally I gave in and told her the truth. As I slept, Delilah cut off my hair. When I awoke, my strength was gone!

Once again the Philistines bound me, but this time I couldn't escape. A servant boy led me into the banquet hall where the evil lords were feasting. Bound between the two pillars supporting the temple, I prayed to God, "Please give me a second chance!"

My hair had begun to grow again and I felt the strength of God returning to my body. I pushed against those pillars and shook them until they crashed to the ground, killing everyone in the room. I died, too, but I thank God that He forgave me and allowed me to make up for my past mistakes.

Guess who?

maximum capacity: 3000 evil lords

BEAUTY IN THE FIELDS

After our husbands died, things weren't easy for my sister-in-law, Orpah, or for myself. We were fortunate that our mother-in-law, Naomi, was a good, kind woman.

Life was so hard in Moab that Naomi decided to return to her home of Bethlehem. Orpah stayed behind, but I went with Naomi. I loved her dearly and would have followed her anywhere.

Naomi had a wealthy relative named Boaz, and it was to his estate that we traveled. I began immediately to glean and gather the sheaves (6) in his barley fields.

As I worked, a dark shadow fell over me. Startled, I looked up into the kind face of a great lord. I bowed my head to hide my flushed cheeks. He told me to stay close to the reapers and they would help to make my work easier. They drew water for me from earthen vessels.

When I told Naomi about the kind lord, she cried, "That was Boaz, my relative! And you say he noticed you! But of course, why shouldn't he—a beautiful girl like you! What a perfect husband he would make!"

One night I lay down at the feet of Boaz while he slept beneath his blanket. In thanks for my loyalty, he gave me six measures of barley (6).

When Boaz asked me to marry him, I was so happy! The only person happier was Naomi. She laughed and cried all at once! Who would have thought that a poor girl, without anyone in the world except her mother-in-law, could find such happiness?

Guess who?

THE JEALOUS KING

I could hear the crowds cheering me. Trumpets (8) blew, tambourines shook, and women danced in my honor. I had killed Goliath.

Little did I know how jealous King Saul had become. At night when he couldn't sleep, he would call for me to play on my harp and to sing. Then he would stare at me with the eyes of a vulture. One night he picked up a javelin and threw it at me. I knew then that it was time to escape.

From that day on, I was a fugitive, forced to live in caves and sleep on stones. Other outcasts joined my band. Then Saul and his army came to fight me on the rocky hills where the wild goats lived.

That night Abishai and I snuck into the camp where Saul slept. "Kill him!" my men advised me. I looked down at the defenseless king. How easy it would be!

At last I whispered, "I can't do it!" Instead, I took his spear and water jug. The next morning I showed him the spear and the jug and said, "I was in your camp last night and could have killed you! Why do you hunt me when I have done you no harm?"

When King Saul heard my words, he felt ashamed. "Forgive me," he cried. "May you be blessed. One day you will wear my crown."

I could have killed Saul. But because I controlled my anger, God blessed me. I became a wise king and learned never to give in to revenge.

Guess who?

CHARIOTS OF FIRE

It isn't easy being a servant of the Lord. Evil kings  and false prophets always want to kill me !

One such man was the king of Aram . His big dream was to destroy Israel—and me along with it. But time after time his secret plans were thwarted. "Which one of you is betraying me?" he would roar, his face tomato- red.

One of his servants explained that it was really *my* fault. "That man of God tells the king of Israel your most secret plans—even the ones you speak in your bedroom!"

The king of Aram was really angry now. When his spies discovered that I lived in Dothan, he sent an army with horses (9) and chariots to seize me in the night.

My servant nearly fainted when he saw the flashing steel of swords and shields surrounding the city. The poor man should have known better than to be afraid. "Just look over there," I told him, pointing to the hills. God opened his eyes and he saw a heavenly army in chariots of fire .

Then I prayed to God, "Strike Aram's army with blindness!" Immediately they became blind and began tripping and bumping into each other. They didn't know which way to go, so I led them right into the camp of the Israelites.

The king of Israel wanted to have them killed, but I said, "Feed them bread and water and send them back. The Lord has done a good thing today."

Guess who?

DETERMINED TO SUCCEED

Even though I was a captive Jew in the land of Persia, I had worked my way up to an important position. I was the official cupbearer to King Artaxerxes himself.

Every evening while Artaxerxes sat with the queen , I brought him his wine on a silver tray . On one occasion, I couldn't hide my sadness. "My beloved Jerusalem, with the tombs of my ancestors, has been destroyed," I told him.

I could hardly believe it when he gave me permission to repair the city! Armed with horsemen and with official letters , I started on my journey. Asaph , the keeper of the king's forest, gave me wooden beams to rebuild the gates.

When I arrived, everyone was willing to help with the repairs, except for Sanballat and Tobiah . Word reached me that they planned to lead an attack on the workers.

"Never!" I roared. "Not after all our hard work!" I ordered the people: "In one hand hold your tools and in the other your swords , spears , bows , and shields . I will post lookouts with trumpets to warn us of an attack."

Thankfully, we finished our repairs at last. With singers and cymbals and harps , we held a huge feast and dedicated the city to the Lord. How glad I was that I hadn't given up! God gave me the strength and determination to finish my job. He gave me the ability to succeed!

Guess who?

A SPECIAL CHILD

From the moment the angel announced my son's birth, I felt happy and blessed, but I knew that it wouldn't be easy to be the mother of such a special child.

When our boy was 12, Joseph and I took him to Jerusalem to celebrate the feast of the Passover. After the celebration was over, we joined a huge caravan and headed for home. It was difficult to keep track of everyone in the confusion. Friends ran back and forth, talking and laughing. Donkeys (6) brayed and horses neighed. Camels (5) complained under the weight of pots and pans and folded tents and other supplies.

When night fell, I realized that my son was missing! What had happened? Had he been attacked by wild animals, killed by bandits?

Joseph and I had no choice but to return to Jerusalem. For three days we searched and searched. At last we looked in the temple. Imagine our surprise when we saw our son sitting and talking with the teachers. And not only that—it was *he* who was teaching *them*!

I took him outside and scolded him. "How could you do this to us?" I cried. My young son said without apology, "Why were you concerned? Didn't you realize I must obey my Father?"

I looked down at him in frustration. Why, oh why, couldn't he just be ordinary, like other children? But I knew that wasn't possible. I prayed that one day I would understand. Until then, I would be the best mother I could.

Guess who?

A FOOL FOR THE LORD

Day after day I  sat on the highway leading to Jericho, a poor blind man begging for pennies (7) and bits of bread. How I wished that Jesus would pass by and heal me. God must have heard my prayer because one day Jesus, with Peter and John, came walking down the very road where I sat. The crowd following him was so huge that I couldn't squeeze through.

I knew that I had to do something fast, or I would lose my chance to be healed. I stood up and started shouting, "Jesus, Son of David, have mercy on me!" People began telling me to be quiet. "You're behaving like a lunatic!" they said. But I didn't care. At least I was being noticed!

Finally Jesus heard the commotion. "Send him here," he commanded. The same people who had been telling me to be quiet, now said in sweet, syrupy voices, "Please, calm down. Let us help you."

I threw off my cloak and ran to meet Jesus. When he asked, "What do you want of me?" I said in a shaking voice, "I want to see."

Jesus answered, "Your faith has healed you."

In that instant, my eyes were opened! I was so happy, so excited, so thankful, that I ran after Jesus all the way down the road. I didn't care that I'd made a fool of myself, yelling at the top of my voice. All that mattered was that Jesus had heard me and had answered my prayers!

Guess who?

WHO IS MY NEIGHBOR

Jesus  must have been the greatest storyteller of all time. Here is a story He told about me …

Once there was a man who was traveling from Jerusalem to Jericho. A band of robbers attacked him and beat him and stole the clothes off his back. Then they tossed him by the side of the road and left him for dead.

Soon a priest came walking by. When he saw the wounded man, he quickly crossed over to the other side of the road. "How disgusting!" he thought. The priest was far too holy to help. He didn't want to dirty his hands or his pure white robe .

As the afternoon sun grew hot, a wealthy Levite came along. He inspected the wounded man with curiosity, holding his handkerchief over his nose and swatting at the flies . Then he continued on his way.

It was late afternoon before I arrived. When I saw the poor man, I washed his wounds with oil and wine and put him on my donkey . I took him to an inn and gave the innkeeper two denarii to take care of the man until I returned.

Jesus finished the story by saying, "Which one of the three men was a good neighbor to the wounded man?"

Of course the answer was obvious. It was me!

Guess who?

BACK FROM THE DEAD

My brother Lazarus  was so sick that my sister Martha and I were afraid he would die. We sent word to Jesus to come quickly. We were sure He would hurry to help Lazarus.

We waited and waited. In despair we watched our brother suffer... and finally die. Why hadn't Jesus answered our call? My handkerchief was wet with tears and my eyes were red with crying.

Looking out the window, I saw a messenger hurrying toward our house. Grabbing my sandals and my veil , I ran out to meet him. "Jesus is coming," he panted. Off I ran down the road. Falling at Jesus' feet, I sobbed, "If only You'd been here, my brother wouldn't have died!"

Word had reached Martha of Jesus' arrival and she came to meet Him with many of the mourners . When Jesus saw them crying, He began to cry as well. "Lead me to the tomb ," He said.

To our astonishment, Jesus ordered the stone in front of the tomb rolled away. I explained that Lazarus had been dead four days—the smell would be terrible.

Jesus said, "Didn't I tell you that if you would believe, you would see the glory of God?" Then He cried in a loud voice, "Lazarus, come out!"

Oh, the joy, the terror, the wonder I felt when I saw my brother, wrapped in grave clothes , walk out of the tomb!

I now know that Jesus answered our prayers at just the right moment, even though it hadn't been when we had wanted.

Guess who?

BETTER THAN GOLD

Life was very exciting for those of us who started the first church. We traveled everywhere, preaching the gospel and healing the sick. In one day about 3000 people became disciples of the risen Lord!

One afternoon Peter 🪨 and I 🖐️ decided to go to the temple to pray. On our way, we had to push through the crowds of people going back and forth to sacrifice their doves 🕊️ and their sheep 🐑. As we passed through the Gate Beautiful 🏛️, someone called out to us, "Alms for the poor. A few pennies 🪙 for a beggar 😣!"

We looked down to see a crippled man 🧎, holding up his bowl 🥣 toward us. Peter called to him, "Look at us."

He looked up hopefully, expecting to be given some money 💵, or perhaps a bit of bread 🍞 or cheese 🧀

But Peter said, "We have no silver 🥢 or gold 💰, but something much better. In the name of Jesus Christ, get up and walk!" Reaching down, Peter took the astonished man by the hand. Immediately he stood up and began jumping and singing and praising God. He danced all the way to the temple where he thanked God for His mercy.

👒 Everyone in the street—from the priests and the teachers 🎓, right on down to the beggar children 🧒 playing in the gutter—had known who the cripple was. They listened eagerly as Peter and I told them of the healing power of Jesus. When we reached the temple, our prayers were filled with thanksgiving for God's goodness!

Guess who?

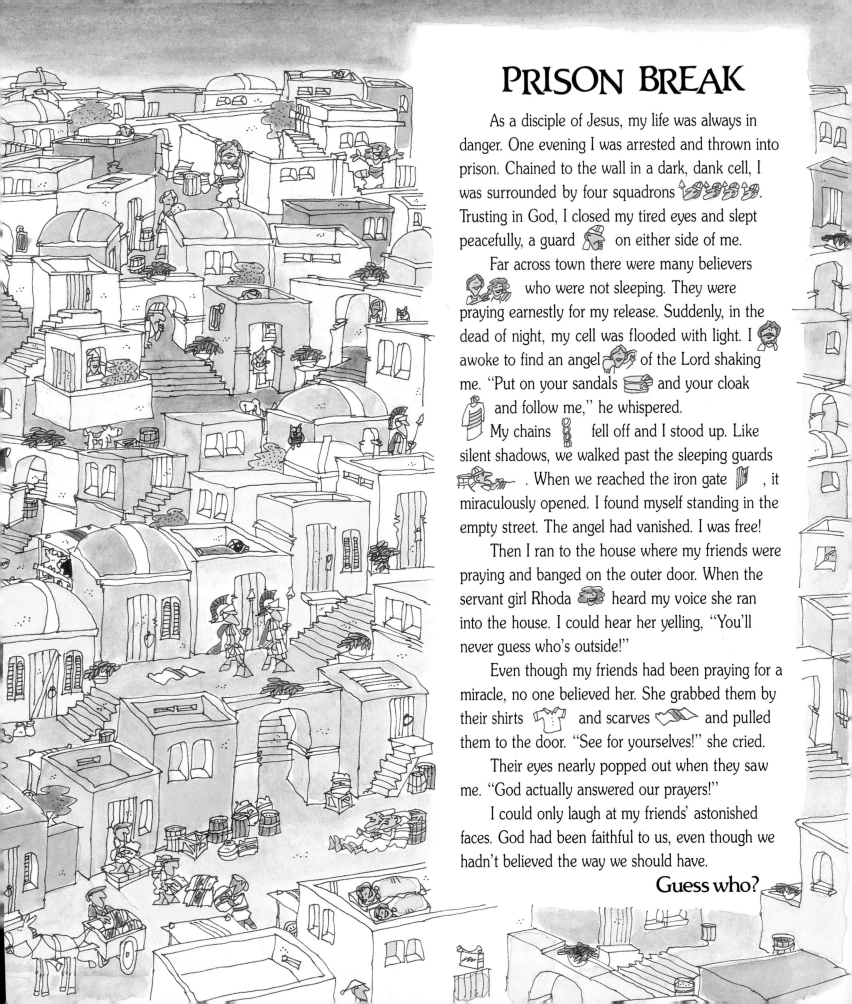

PRISON BREAK

As a disciple of Jesus, my life was always in danger. One evening I was arrested and thrown into prison. Chained to the wall in a dark, dank cell, I was surrounded by four squadrons. Trusting in God, I closed my tired eyes and slept peacefully, a guard on either side of me.

Far across town there were many believers who were not sleeping. They were praying earnestly for my release. Suddenly, in the dead of night, my cell was flooded with light. I awoke to find an angel of the Lord shaking me. "Put on your sandals and your cloak and follow me," he whispered.

My chains fell off and I stood up. Like silent shadows, we walked past the sleeping guards. When we reached the iron gate, it miraculously opened. I found myself standing in the empty street. The angel had vanished. I was free!

Then I ran to the house where my friends were praying and banged on the outer door. When the servant girl Rhoda heard my voice she ran into the house. I could hear her yelling, "You'll never guess who's outside!"

Even though my friends had been praying for a miracle, no one believed her. She grabbed them by their shirts and scarves and pulled them to the door. "See for yourselves!" she cried.

Their eyes nearly popped out when they saw me. "God actually answered our prayers!"

I could only laugh at my friends' astonished faces. God had been faithful to us, even though we hadn't believed the way we should have.

Guess who?

MISSIONARY JOURNEYS

Over the years, I 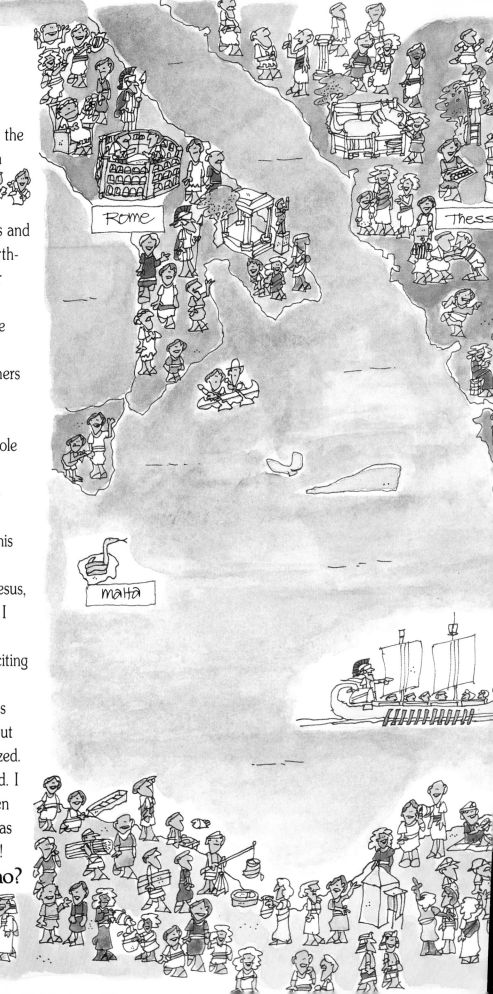 have tried to reach the whole world with the gospel. My journeys with Barnabas, Silas, Mark, and Timothy have led to many exciting adventures.

I remember the time in Philippi when Silas and I were captured and put in prison. A violent earthquake shook the ground and freed us from our chains.

In Thessalonica we spoke in the synagogue and many Greeks and Jews believed in Jesus. But there were others who were jealous. They stirred up an evil mob and we barely escaped.

When I reached Athens, I saw that the whole city worshiped idols. At the altar inscribed "To an Unknown God," I started to preach about Jesus, the true God.

In Corinth I stayed with Aquila and his wife Priscilla and sewed tents.

I went many other places as well—to Ephesus, Galatia, Colossae, and Jerusalem. In Jerusalem I was arrested and sent to Rome by Festus. My journey to Rome was probably the most exciting of all. We were shipwrecked on the island of Malta. As I built a fire a poisonous snake came out of the flames. It bit me, but didn't harm me. The islanders were amazed.

I am now in Rome, waiting to be sentenced. I don't know what the future holds—perhaps even death. But I am happy just knowing that God has brought me here. I will continue to trust in Him!

Guess who?

Philippi

Galatia

Colossae

Athens

Corinth

Ephesus

Mediterranean Sea

Sea of Galilee

Egypt

Jerusalem

WHO AM I

I live in a yellow house  at the end of a shady street, just outside the big city. But I suppose I could live anywhere—in a high-rise apartment, in a small town, on a farm, or even in a cabin in the woods.

I love my mom, my dad, my little sister (she's crazy), and my dog (he's even crazier). Every day the bus picks me up and takes me to school. Sometimes I'm late and I forget my backpack and my lunch and I put my shirt on backwards. Those are the bad days. But most of the time I manage to get to school on time and with everything I need. If that isn't a miracle, I don't know what is!

I think I'm pretty ordinary, but there's one thing that makes me different from a lot of other kids: I'm a follower of Jesus, just like the people in this book. I know I'm not a king or a queen, or the leader of a great army—and I'm definitely not strong like Samson. (Maybe I should start lifting weights!)

But I can still be strong for the Lord. When I read the Bible, go to church, and pray I can feel my spiritual muscles growing. Jesus wants me to love my family and to help my friends, my teachers, and my neighbors. But the thing He wants most from me is my heart. He wants me! Do *you* know who I am?

Guess who?

More "Finders" For Seekers...

Looking for *even more* fun? Try your hand at finding the surprises below.
They could be hiding anywhere!

 Chicken dinner

 Bethlehem haircut

 Manhole worker

 Early croquet

 Happy horse

 Dog tricks

 Boy Scout

 Lost miner

 Jericho barbecue

 Lunch break

 Beverage service

 Lost tourists

 Skier

 Ancient ref

 Haran tuba player

 Cat chorale

 Foxy racoon

 Lady losing laundry

 Party favor

 Oops

 Umbrella jumper

 News team

 Gumball machine

 Clever harvester

 Sandcastle

 Happy face

 Water fun

 Hungry squirrel

 Kissing cow

 Bethany newsman

 Escaping chicken

 Sleepy soldier

 Water spill

 Violin serenade

 Old sea captain

Righteous Radical Checklist

Did you guess the right righteous radicals? Check this list to find out. You can read more about their adventures in the Bible verses that go with each story.

Get Up & Get Out!
Abraham
Genesis 11:27–12:20

A Super Man
Samson
Judges 14–16

Beauty in the Fields
Ruth
Book of Ruth

The Jealous King
David
1 Samuel 18:5-16 (background)
1 Samuel 26 (story)

Chariots of Fire
Elisha
2 Kings 6:8-23

Determined to Succeed
Nehemiah
Book of Nehemiah

A Special Child
(Jesus at 12 years old)
Mary the mother of Jesus
Luke 2:39-52

A Fool for the Lord
Bartimaeus
Mark 10:46-52

Who Is My Neighbor?
The Good Samaritan
Luke 10:25-37

Back from the Dead
Mary the sister of Lazarus
John 11:1-44

Better Than Gold
John
Acts 3:1-10

Prison Break
Peter
Acts 12:1-17

Missionary Journeys
Paul
Acts 13:1-28:31

Who Am I?
A Right-Now Righteous Radical—someone like you!
John 3:16
John 1:12

"You will seek me and find me
when you seek me with all your heart,"
declares the Lord.

—Jeremiah 29:13

Library of Congress Cataloging-in-Publication Data

Mezek, Karen, 1956-
In search of righteous radicals
illustrated by Sandy Silverthorne ; retold by Karen Mezek.
Summary: Presents stories from the Old and New Testaments
about "righteous radicals" whose identity the reader is to guess.
Gives a related devotional thought for each story.
ISBN 0-89081-986-6
1. Bible stories, English.   2. Children—Prayer books and devotions—English.
[1. Bible stories.   2. Literary recreations.]
I. Silverthorne, Sandy, 1951-   ill.   II. Title.
BS551.2M44   1992
220.9'505—dc90   91-45596
                                    CIP
                                    AC

Printed in the United States of America.